Sally Ride

America's First Woman
In Space

Sally Ride

America's First Woman
In Space

by Carolyn Blacknall

DILLON PRESS, INC. MINNEAPOLIS, MINNESOTA

The photographs are reproduced through the courtesy of Joyce Ride and the National Aeronautics and Space Administration.

Library of Congress Cataloging in Publication Data

Blacknall, Carolyn.
    Sally Ride : America's first woman in space.

    (Taking Part)
    SUMMARY: A biography of Sally Ride, who in 1983 became the first American woman in space.
    1. Ride, Sally—Juvenile literature. 2. Astronauts—United States—Biography—Juvenile literature.
    [1. Ride, Sally. 2. Astronauts] I. Title
    TL789.85.R53B53   1984   629.45′0092′4 [B]   [92]   84-12671

    ISBN 0-87518-260-7 (lib. bdg.)

© 1984 by Dillon Press, Inc. All rights reserved

Dillon Press, Inc., 242 Portland Avenue South
Minneapolis, Minnesota 55415

Printed in the United States of America
                5 6 7 8 9 10 91 90 89 88 87

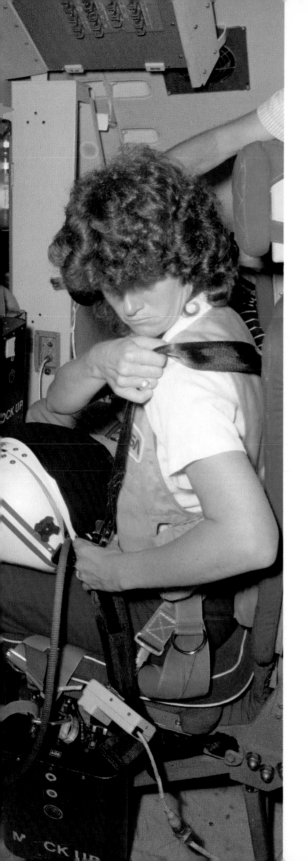

Contents

Sally Ride

On June 18, 1983, Sally Ride soared into the Florida sky aboard the space shuttle orbiter *Challenger* and made history as America's first woman in space. Along with astronaut John Fabian, she helped launch satellites for Canada and Indonesia and conduct complex scientific experiments. She also helped demonstrate, for the first time, the ability of the shuttle's remote manipulator arm to deploy and retrieve a satellite in space. When *Challenger* landed on June 24 at Edwards Air Force Base in California, the flight of STS-7 was judged a big success. To all Americans, and especially to women, Sally Ride was a national hero.

Sally grew up in Southern California, where she played softball with the neighborhood boys and became a nationally ranked junior tennis player. An excellent student, she attended Swarthmore College and Stanford University. After nine years of study, she had earned degrees in physics and English from Stanford and was about to receive a doctor's degree in astrophysics. She was looking for a job in space research when she noticed a NASA ad for astronauts in the school paper.

In 1978 Dr. Sally K. Ride was one of the 35 astronauts chosen from a group of more than 8,000 men and women who applied to become space shuttle pilots and mission specialists. She completed her training as a mission specialist and was named to the crew of the STS-7 flight. A few months after the successful mission, Sally Ride was assigned to the crew of an early 1985 shuttle flight. Meanwhile, she spends some of her earthbound time speaking to groups in the United States and around the world. Everywhere she goes, Sally encourages girls and young women to become scientists and astronauts. "Because now there really is a way," she says. "Now it's possible."

1/A Time to Explore

Almost half a million people waited along the sandy beaches of Cape Canaveral, Florida. A million eyes strained to see the telltale sign on a distant launch pad. On that crisp morning of June 18, 1983, a sudden hush fell over the huge crowd. Radios counted off the seconds until the launch of the seventh space shuttle flight. Not since the first shuttle mission two years earlier had so many people gathered to watch a lift-off.

The main reason for their attention was not the gleaming white *Challenger* spacecraft. The crowds had come to cheer Sally Ride, soon to become America's first woman in space. This very smart and highly trained young astronaut was about to become a pioneer in one of the many new fields open to women. For Sally, though, flying in space was just the latest of many challenges she had taken on during her 32 years on earth.

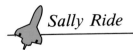

Sally Kristen Ride was born on May 26, 1951, in Los Angeles, California. At that time there weren't any astronauts or spaceships. As Sally grew up, she didn't think about being an astronaut because no one had ever been launched into space before.

Sally did think about sports, though. When she was five years old, she would wake up early, her bright blue eyes shining with excitement. She would race her father to the sidewalk to pick up the morning newspaper. Then she would run back into the family's large, comfortable den and curl up on the couch. Sally would look through all the sections of the paper until she found the sports news. That way she could read the sports pages all by herself.

More than anything else, Sally liked to play ball games with the other children in the neighborhood. The warm, sunny weather in California was great for being outdoors. All year long, Sally enjoyed baseball, softball, football, soccer, and other outdoor sports.

Softball was Sally's favorite sport. The freckle-faced little girl would spend many hours playing softball with other children in the park. Sometimes she was playing with boys only. But Sally didn't mind because she was one of the best players. When the kids divided into teams, she was always the first to be chosen. Often, she was the only girl the boys would allow to play.

Next to sports, Sally liked reading best. She enjoyed mysteries and action stories and spent many happy hours reading to her younger sister Karen. Sally called her "Bear" because she couldn't say "Karen" when the two sisters were very young.

Sally's father, Dale Ride, was a political science teacher at Santa Monica College. At one time her mother, Joyce, had been a teacher. When her two daughters were young, she stayed home to care for them. Sometimes Joyce did volunteer work at the Encino Presbyterian Church, where she and Dale are now elders, or lay leaders. Later she worked as a volunteer counselor at a nearby women's prison.

In many ways the Rides, said Sally's friend, Molly Tyson, "were not a normal family. They didn't have to sit at the same table for dinner. People ate dinner when they wanted, and they could have a whole dinner of nuts and cheese and crackers." If Sally and Bear were tired at the

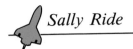

end of a busy day, they didn't have to clean their rooms. No one cared much if the house became cluttered when everyone was busy.

Dale and Joyce Ride didn't place a great deal of importance on housework or other everyday chores. They believed in giving their daughters freedom to try out new things and ideas. "We might have encouraged," said Dale, "but mostly we let them explore." And as Joyce remembered, it wasn't easy to get headstrong Sally to do anything she didn't want to do.

Once Joyce Ride tried to force her oldest daughter to take piano lessons. Sally didn't want to learn to play the piano, and she refused to cooperate with her teacher. Even today, Sally will not play the piano.

Sally did enjoy the people from faraway lands who often came to her home. Dale Ride's job made him interested in the governments and people of other nations. Joyce Ride taught English to foreign students. Whenever they could, they invited foreign visitors to come over for dinner and friendly conversation. From these guests, Sally and Bear learned about the customs, languages, and religions of other lands.

When Sally was nine years old, the Ride family had the chance to learn even more about the people of other nations. That year Dale Ride took a leave of absence, or sabbatical, from his job at Santa Monica College. Dale, Joyce, Sally, and Bear spent the time in Europe. They learned about the governments, schools, and ways of life of several European countries.

For Sally and her sister, traveling in foreign nations was great fun. There were always new sights to see and explore, new people to meet, and new foods to eat. On one day the two girls would climb castle steps and learn about kings and queens and royal families. On the next they would walk through the narrow streets of a city whose history was centuries old. In Yugoslavia, Sally and Bear met a large, friendly collie named *Psigane*, or Gypsy. The girls played with the collie every day until they had to leave the country.

At last the year in Europe came to an end, and the Rides moved back to California. They bought a large house with a big backyard in the city of Encino near Los Angeles. One day Dale and Joyce brought home a beautiful collie puppy and gave it to the two girls. Sally named it

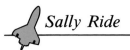

Psigane for the dog that had been their friend in Yugoslavia.

Going to school in Encino was not as exciting as traveling in Europe, but Sally soon found something new and challenging to do. When Joyce and Dale Ride started playing tennis, they bought Sally a racket. Before long Sally began to practice each day. She pounded tennis balls against the garage door and challenged people to play against her on the court. She liked the game so much that she played whenever she could. Sally didn't care whether she was playing against a girl, a boy, or a grown-up. She just wanted to play tennis.

2/Science and Shakespeare

When Sally was eleven, she started taking tennis lessons from Alice Marble, a four-time women's national champion. Every year, Sally's playing improved. After years of practice, she became one of the best junior tennis players in the United States. She was so good that Westlake, a private girls' high school in Los Angeles, offered her a scholarship. Sally, who was also an excellent student, decided to go there.

By the time Sally was at Westlake, she had become a remarkable athlete. Once, her high school teacher tried to show the difference between the heartbeat of a person resting and a person exercising. Usually someone who has been exercising has a much faster heartbeat. The teacher measured how fast Sally's heart was beating in the classroom. Then he asked Sally to run around the Westlake campus. When she ran back into the classroom,

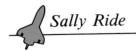

he measured her heartbeat again. Everyone in the class was amazed to find out that Sally's heartbeat was almost unchanged!

At Westlake Sally was an honor student. "But if she was bored in the classroom . . . she would not make an effort," Joyce Ride remembered. "It irritated some teachers. One saw her as a clock-watcher. That was the one exception. The class was dull, and Sally was bored."

Some of the student activities at Westlake bored Sally, too. She didn't join any school clubs or take part in school social groups. Sally placed a high value on being independent and wanted to choose activities that really interested her. Small talk at school parties didn't rate very high on her list of things to do.

One teacher at Westlake introduced Sally to a subject that caught her interest right away. The teacher was Dr. Elizabeth Mommaerts, and the subject was science. From the beginning, Sally was fascinated by the approach Mommaerts used to solve problems. This approach, explained her teacher, was called the scientific method. Using it, a scientist could find the answers to difficult questions.

Sally saw that Elizabeth Mommaerts was a very intelligent, clear-thinking, independent-minded person. Never before in her life had she known a person quite like Dr. Mommaerts. Sally admired her and tried to model her own actions after those of her teacher. Like Mommaerts, she tried to think clearly and approach problems as a scientist would.

Sally's interest in science led to an interest in the stars and space travel. The 1960s, when Sally was in her teens, was an exciting time for America's space program. President John Kennedy had pledged the United States to the goal of sending an astronaut to the moon by 1970.

Like other American families, the Rides were proud of the achievements of American astronauts. They watched as the early Project Mercury flights launched men in space capsules. Later they followed the Project Gemini program, which put crews of two men into space for longer periods. Sally learned that the first astronauts were all test pilots from the armed services.

On July 10, 1969, many millions of people around the world watched TV pictures of the *Apollo 11* astronauts on the moon. Sally was then 18 years old. As she looked

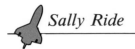

at the first men on the moon, she wondered what it would be like to travel in space. There were still no women astronauts, but many of the space men were now scientists instead of jet pilots.

In high school Elizabeth Mommaerts had shown her some of the excitement of being a scientist. Sally decided to study all the sciences she could in college. Though she didn't think she would ever be an astronaut, she thought she would enjoy studying about space.

Sally started her studies at Swarthmore College in Pennsylvania. In her first college years, she studied only mathematics and science. Her favorite subjects were astronomy — the study of all objects in space — and physics. Sally learned to go straight to the heart of each problem she was given. Once more, she received excellent grades.

While Sally was at Swarthmore, both sports and science were important to her. A reporter called her the best female college tennis player in the East. In the same article, Sally said she would like to work in space research and "hopes she has what it takes to make a space team."

Fred Hargadon, who was then dean of admissions at

Swarthmore, knew about Sally's interest in space, too. He remembers what happened when he interviewed her in Los Angeles. "We were sitting outside at dusk and Sally was explaining the constellations [groups of stars] to me. I had no idea whether she knew what she was talking about, but I was struck by how bright she was."

After a year and a half in Pennsylvania, Sally became homesick for her sunny home state. She left Swarthmore and returned to California to attend Stanford University.

At Stanford, Sally added English classes to her schedule. "I needed a break from the equations," she later admitted. Sally had discovered that there was more to college life than just math and science.

Some of her English classes were supposed to have class discussions. When it was Sally's turn to lead the class, she didn't want to waste time talking. Her style was to think of a few key statements and then explain them to the class so well that there was no need to continue the discussion.

In the English department, Sally's special field of study was Shakespeare. William Shakespeare was an English author who lived several hundred years ago.

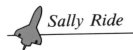

Today he is known all over the world for the fine plays he wrote and staged in England. "I really had fun reading Shakespeare's plays and writing papers on them," Sally said later. "It's kind of like doing puzzles. You had to figure out what he was trying to say and find all the little clues inside the play [to prove] that you were right." Sally could find just the right clues to explain what Shakespeare was saying.

Along with Shakespeare and science studies, Sally still played in many kinds of sports. One was rugby, a hard-hitting sport much like football. And nearly every day, she would compete in a fast-paced tennis game.

In 1972, tennis star Billie Jean King—one of the game's greatest players—watched Sally in a tennis match. She suggested that Sally quit school and become a professional tennis player. Sally knew that she could be a good tennis player, but she also believed that she could be an even better space scientist. Finally, after thinking about all the pros and cons, Sally made up her mind. She decided to stay in college.

Why didn't Sally take Billy Jean King's advice and become a pro tennis player? According to Sally, "I had a bad forehand." Joyce Ride said of her daughter: "She stopped playing tennis because she couldn't make the ball go just where she wanted it to." "Sally is very competitive," said her father. "She knows what she can do, and she likes to win." Perhaps Karen "Bear" Ride explained Sally's important decision the best. "She doesn't run around trying to make everyone happy," Karen said of her sister. "Sally lives up to her own standards. What other people think of her is not of ultimate importance to her."

Sally's tennis game did not measure up to the standards of excellence she had set for herself. She gave up the idea of being a pro player to concentrate on an area where she could achieve her own goals—the study of science and Shakespeare.

Molly Tyson, Sally's roommate and friend at Stanford, remembered how serious Sally was about her studies. "She never got less than an *A* in English. She wrote English papers the way she wrote science papers," said Molly. "She would turn in three pages, and that was it. But she would always see to the heart of things."

Sally's college life was not all hard work and study. She and Molly did some fun things together, too. Some-

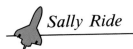

times they would go out with girlfriends for a drive through the California countryside. Returning to their dusty apartment, they often faced a pile of dirty dishes by the sink. Sally's housecleaning habits hadn't improved much since she left home.

Like most college students, Sally and Molly had trouble eating regular meals every day. Usually the two roommates would try to eat a balanced diet of healthy foods. Once in a while, though, they would lose their will power and just eat hamburgers and french fries for days at a time.

Life at college, away from her parents, helped prepare Sally for solving problems on her own. One evening when Sally and Molly were out for a ride, a hose broke in Sally's car. Soon all the water in the radiator sprayed out. The two young women were stranded on an empty road. Molly wanted to wait for help. In the meantime, Sally managed to find the break and fix it with a roll of Scotch tape. Then she found some water in a nearby stream and used an old saucepan to refill her radiator. Less than an hour after the break, the car was running again.

3/Dr. Sally Ride, Astronaut

By 1973, Sally had earned a lot of college credits in English and science. She hadn't decided exactly what she wanted to do next. That spring Sally Ride graduated from Stanford with a degree in English and a degree in physics.

In the fall, Sally continued studying physics in graduate school at Stanford. Because of her interest in space, she also took many astronomy classes. One of her strong areas of interest was the X rays given off by distant stars. In graduate school Sally studied some difficult scientific subjects. Like many other graduate students, she helped the professors with their research and in teaching classes.

Sally Ride spent nine years in college. She was about to leave Stanford with a doctor's degree in astrophysics. During her last year there, she began to look around for research jobs in her field.

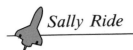

Then Sally saw an advertisement in the Stanford paper. The National Aeronautics and Space Administration (NASA), said the ad, was searching for astronauts for the new space shuttle program. This was the first time in ten years that NASA would be hiring astronauts. Together they would form the eighth group of astronauts ever chosen by the space agency.

NASA wanted some members of the eighth group to be jet pilots. But the others would be a new kind of astronaut. These experts would run experiments and be in charge of the shuttle's cargo, or payloads. They would be called mission specialists. NASA wanted the best scientists, engineers, and medical doctors for this job—men and women.

Sally was delighted. "I don't know why I wanted to do it," she said later. "I never had any burning ambition to be in the space program . . . I never even thought about how they recruited astronauts. When I saw them on TV, they all seemed to be Navy or Air Force test pilots. I suppose I just took it for granted that it was pretty much a closed club."

Now that closed club was about to open its doors to

some new and eager members—the women of America. It would never be the same again.

Sally filled out the forms to be a mission specialist and mailed them to the Johnson Space Center in Houston. More than 7,000 men and 1,000 women also applied to be in this eighth astronaut group. Officials at NASA read through all the forms. They picked out the people with the best grades in college. They also chose top-notch scientists, engineers, doctors, and pilots. At last 208 men and women—including Dr. Sally Ride—were chosen as finalists. From these, NASA would select the best 35 to be astronauts.

NASA invited all the finalists to visit the Johnson Space Center. Each person had to answer many questions. Some questions were asked to find out who would stay calm in emergencies. The finalists also took running and exercising tests to show if they were in good physical condition.

In January 1978, NASA announced that the 35 people in the eighth astronaut group had been chosen. Fifteen were selected to be space shuttle pilots. Twenty were chosen as mission specialists, and six of the mission specialists were women. One of them was Dr. Sally Ride. "Now I'm so excited," Sally said, "I'd like to go up [in space] tomorrow!"

The 35 people in Sally's group were called astronaut candidates. If they could complete one year of training, they would become full-fledged astronauts.

All the astronaut candidates moved to Houston for their training. Reporters talked with many members of the new group, but they were most interested in the six women who would study to be mission specialists. Since American women had never been astronauts before, the newspeople wanted to find out everything about them.

Some reporters asked Sally what qualities she had that would make her a good astronaut. She smiled and said, "A good educational background and one that showed I could learn things readily."

Sally Ride went to interviews and posed for group pictures with the five other women. Soon, though, she became tired of all the attention. She didn't like answering the same questions over and over again. Sally tried to avoid questions about her home life because she wanted to stay a private person.

As an astronaut candidate, Sally wanted to spend her time training to fly in space. The eighth group of astronauts had a lot to learn. Much of their training would be in classes at the Johnson Space Center in Houston. They would have classes in mathematics, meteorology, astronomy, navigation, physics, and computers.

The new astronauts would also learn about the three parts of the Space Transportation System, or STS. The largest part was the huge, 154-foot tank that would hold the fuel burned during launch by the orbiter's three main engines. A second part was the solid rocket boosters, which would provide the extra power needed for launch. Most of the astronaut candidates' time was spent learning about the main part of STS—the shuttle orbiter. The orbiter, which looked like a stubby, short-winged airplane, would hold the astronauts and cargo on their trips into space.

Officials at NASA knew that even with a year of training, the astronauts could not learn everything about the shuttle. In addition to classes on the basic shuttle systems, they gave each astronaut one part to study in detail. Then, if there were any questions about or changes in that

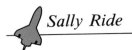
part, the astronaut would give a report to the others.

Sally Ride and John Fabian were both given the remote manipulator system as their special project to study. This jointed, 50-foot-long robot arm would be used to handle cargo in the shuttle's payload bay. One use of the arm would be to release and pick up satellites.

Sally and John made trips to Toronto, Canada, to study the giant arm, which was still being developed. They tested its displays and controls. They even made suggestions about how the arm could be improved.

As a mission specialist, Sally did not have to know how to fly the shuttle. But she did have to learn how the shuttle worked. In space she would have to know how to run experiments and launch satellites from the orbiter's payload bay.

Large models of the orbiter, called shuttle simulators, were used for this training. They had all the lights and instruments found in real orbiters. These displays were run by a computer programmed to make the instruments show the same readings as in a shuttle spaceflight. Views of the earth, payloads, and landing runways were shown on movie screens outside the simulator's windows. Sally spent many hours in these models while she was learning to use the shuttle's controls.

Astronaut candidates had to do more than study hard in their classes. Part of their job was to stay in good physical condition. There were no group exercise classes for the new astronauts. Each person chose his or her own kind of health program.

Sally Ride decided that she would run to stay fit because running didn't take long and she could do it at any time of day. "There is no program as such that we have to follow," she explained, "but I run because it makes me feel better and I enjoy it." Sally set a goal to run four miles a day during the week and eight or ten miles a day on weekends.

In addition to running, Sally still played tennis and volleyball whenever she could. She also took up weight lifting. Sally laughingly said that it helped her carry the 45-pound parachutes used in NASA's T-38 training jets.

One of Sally's favorite parts of training was her flights in NASA's training jets. Each member of their class had to spend 15 hours a month in the jets. Those who were not pilots rode in the back of the planes as copilots.

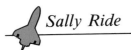

Sally made many trips in T-38 jets. She often flew to the Kennedy Space Center in Florida to study the shuttle launch site. Sometimes she flew to other NASA centers in California, New Mexico, and Alabama. The young mission specialist liked the flights so much that she studied flying and soon earned her own pilot's license.

Sally enjoyed all of her training, even the difficult parts. One of the most challenging parts was learning how to live and work in the almost weightless conditions aboard the space shuttle.

NASA had found a way for the astronauts to practice in these special conditions. To create them, a KC-135 jet was used. The inside of this plane was empty, and all the walls were padded. The jet was flown to a high altitude, and then made to dive straight down before slowly gaining altitude again.

To Sally and the other astronauts, the fast fall felt like being in a falling elevator, or going down a steep roller coaster. For half a minute each time, the astronauts floated weightless inside the jet. Sally practiced eating, drinking, putting on spacesuits, and using shuttle equipment during these short periods without gravity.

In January 1979, the official training period was complete, and all the astronaut candidates became full-fledged astronauts. The new astronauts held a party to celebrate. Now they might be chosen to fly in the space shuttle!

The Ride family: (in front) *Dale Ride, Sally, and Joyce Ride, and* (in back) *Karen "Bear" Ride and her husband.*

(Left) *Sally at the tennis court during her first year in college.*
(Right) *As a new astronaut in 1978, Sally Ride speaks to an audience of high school girls.*

Sally in junior high.

33

Five astronaut candidates take a break from a hard day of training: (from the left) *Sally Ride, Judith Resnik, Anna Fisher, Kathryn Sullivan, and Rhea Seddon.*

Working in a full-scale model of the shuttle's cargo bay, Sally Ride practices moving the remote manipulator arm.

(Left) *Sitting in a model of an airplane cockpit, Sally Ride prepares to learn what it feels like to be ejected, or thrown out of, a plane in an emergency.* (Above) *Astronaut candidate Ride leaves a T-38 jet following a training flight.*

Dr. Sally K. Ride and an aircraft engineer inspect one of the satellites to be carried aboard Challenger *on the seventh space shuttle flight.*

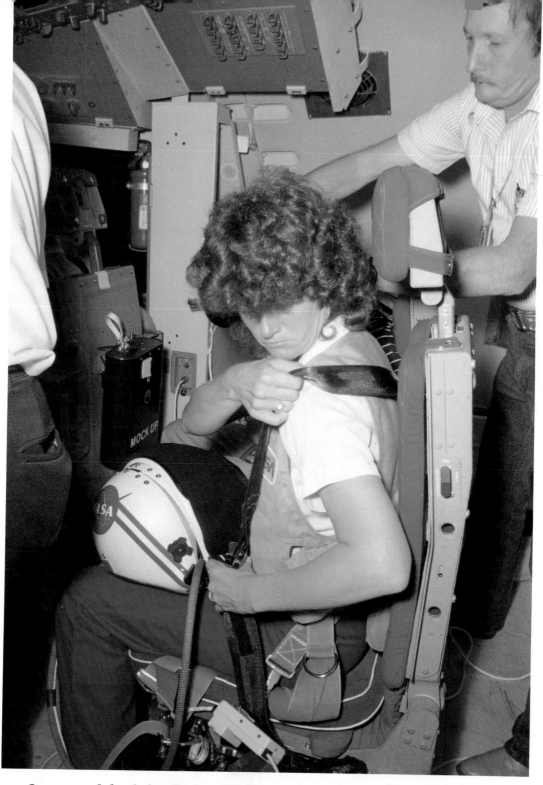

On a model of the flight deck of the space shuttle orbiter, Sally Ride adjusts the shoulder strap of her seat.

The crew for the flight of STS-7: (from the left) Sally Ride, John Fabian, Commander Robert Crippen, Norman Thagard, and Rick Hauck.

Dr. Steven Hawley, Sally Ride's husband and also a mission specialist in the 1978 astronaut group.

4/"The Very Best Person for the Job"

Each astronaut in the eighth group was given a new and important job in the space shuttle program. During the first shuttle flight, STS-1, in April 1981, Sally rode in the back of a T-38 chase plane. The chase planes followed the shuttle from the upper atmosphere down to the landing strip. Astronauts in the planes took pictures and supplied wind and weather information to the crew of the *Columbia*.

After the first shuttle flight, Sally Ride was given another important task. She would serve as one of the capcoms on the second and third shuttle missions. The capcom is a person who fills a key ground control job at the Mission Control Center in Houston. He or she is the only person allowed to talk with a spacecraft during a flight. *Capcom* comes from *capsule communicator*, a term first used when astronauts flew in tiny capsules.

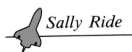

Sally Ride would be the first woman ever to serve in this job.

As capcom, Sally passed on the advice of scientists working in mission control to the astronauts in the shuttle orbiter. Once, when she was serving as capcom during the second shuttle flight, astronauts Joe Engle and Richard Truly told her how beautiful the view was in space. Sally replied, "Sounds good." Then she laughingly asked them, "When do I get my turn?"

Sally's turn would come sooner than she had imagined. In April 1982, NASA announced the crew for STS-7, the seventh shuttle flight. Three of the 1978 astronaut group were chosen for this mission. One of them was Dr. Sally Ride!

The commander of the seventh mission would be Bob Crippen, who had flown on the first shuttle mission almost two years earlier. The pilot would be Rick Hauck. The other mission specialist chosen was John Fabian. He had worked with Sally on developing the remote manipulator arm.

Sally was bubbling with excitement when she called her parents in California. "Sally is normally very cool, very low key," Joyce Ride remembered. "But when she called to tell me the news, she was bordering on breathless."

Five hundred reporters called NASA to talk with Sally Ride. All of them wanted to learn more about the first American spacewoman. NASA brought the reporters together for a press conference so that they could meet Sally and the three other astronauts who would fly with her. The reporters asked many questions about STS-7. But they were most interested in the calm young woman who had been chosen to make space history.

Commander Bob Crippen explained why he wanted Sally Ride in his crew for the mission. "I wanted a competent engineer who was cool under stress. Sally demonstrated that talent. She also has a pleasing personality that will fit in with the group."

Sally beamed as she announced, "It's quite an honor. I'm very honored NASA chose me to be the first woman."

The questions about Sally Ride did not stop with the first press conference. Because she was a woman, the reporters paid more attention to her than anyone else in the STS-7 flight crew. Sally handled all the questions

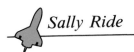

calmly but firmly. "I did not come to NASA to make history," she said. "It's important to me that people don't think I was picked for the flight because I am a woman and it's time for NASA to send one."

Why was Sally Ride really picked to fly on STS-7? George W.S. Abbey, NASA's director of flight operations, was in a good position to know. He said that Sally had shown a strong ability to solve difficult engineering problems. Perhaps even more important, he added, she was a "team player" who worked well with the other astronauts. "Sally Ride is smart in a very special way," explained Abbey. "You get people who can sit in the lab and think like an Einstein [a famous scientist], but they can't do anything with it. Sally can get everything she knows together and bring it to bear where you need it."

Commander Crippen was upset by all the reporters' questions about Sally. Finally he tried to put an end to the pointless questions. "She is flying with us because she is the very best person for the job," said Crippen. "There is no man I would rather have in her place."

Bob Crippen, Sally Ride, and the other STS-7 crew members wanted to get on with the business of preparing for their spaceflight. The four astronauts now moved into a large office together. They would spend the next year working with each other and training for their mission.

Training for one flight was even harder than studying the parts of the Space Transportation System. Instead of learning about space experiments in general, Sally Ride and John Fabian studied in detail all the experiments of STS-7. They also learned about the three satellites that would be launched from the orbiter during the mission.

One of the most important things that the crew members studied was a timeline of the flight. The timeline was the list of all the jobs to be done and when to do them. The astronauts practiced each job many times on the ground so that they wouldn't waste time getting it done in space.

Sally worked hard on her part of the timeline. During much of the mission, she would be performing experiments or using the remote manipulator arm. After a while, she had practiced her jobs so much that she felt she could do them in her sleep.

The many reporters had not lost interest in Sally Ride. They took pictures of her working with the STS-7

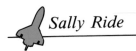

experiments and operating the giant robot arm. They even tried to take pictures of her at home.

Sally wanted to keep her personal life private. Away from her job, she tried to keep the reporters at a safe distance. At that time she had a special reason for wanting them to stay away.

Sally had been dating Steven Hawley, another member of NASA's eighth astronaut group. Like Sally, the blond, blue-eyed young man had studied astronomy in college before being selected as an astronaut.

In July 1982, Steve and Sally decided to get married. To keep their plans private, they told only their relatives and a few of their closest friends. The wedding was held at Steve's parents' home in Salina, Kansas. To get there quickly, Sally flew a jet plane from Houston to Kansas. During the short ceremony, the bride wore blue jeans and a rugby shirt. Two ministers took part in the wedding— Dr. Bernard Hawley, Steven's father, and Karen "Bear" Scott, who had married and was now a Presbyterian minister.

Afterward, Sally and Steve returned to their work at the Johnson Space Center. Much of Sally's time was now spent practicing each step of the STS-7 mission. She and the other members of the crew acted out the flight together in a shuttle simulator model. Unlike earlier tests, the ground control teams took their places in the Mission Control Center and practiced with the crew.

During the one year of training for the flight, NASA officials were observing astronauts working on other shuttle missions. They noticed that about half of the astronauts were "space sick" for part of their time in space. A spacewalk on the fifth shuttle mission had to be delayed because of space sickness.

NASA made a decision to add a doctor to the crew of STS-7 to study the causes of space sickness. Dr. Norm Thagard, another mission specialist from the eighth astronaut group, was chosen for this job. Dr. Thagard worked closely with the rest of the crew as they prepared for their flight. With him on board, STS-7 would be the first American spaceflight with five crew members.

5/"Ride, Sally Ride"

Problems in the testing of *Challenger,* the new shuttle orbiter, delayed the STS-7 launch. At last, in summer 1983, launch week arrived.

Three days before lift-off, the five astronauts arrived in their T-38 jets at the Kennedy Space Center in Florida. They were kept apart from other people to avoid becoming sick. To prepare for their morning launch time, they ate special meals and woke up earlier each day.

On Saturday, June 18, the STS-7 crew woke up at quarter past three in the morning. After breakfast, the astronauts rode in a small van to launch pad 39-A. When they arrived, the first rays of sunrise lit the Space Transportation System in shades of pink and violet. Sally looked at the four and a half million pound spacecraft towering over 150 feet in the air. Everyone was quiet for a moment.

Commander Bob Crippen led the way into the nearby white room, where the astronauts dressed and prepared to enter the orbiter. To keep dust out of STS-7, the white room was cleaner than an operating room in a hospital.

An hour and a half before launch, the crew left the white room and entered the space shuttle. Bob Crippen and pilot Rick Hauck took their seats at the front of the flight deck. Sally Ride and John Fabian went to their places behind them. Norm Thagard would ride below the others in the mid-deck section of the orbiter.

The radio crackled with a last-minute message from Steve Hawley. "Sally, have a ball!" her husband said.

Fifteen minutes before lift-off, scientists at the launch control center in Florida checked the instruments that reported on STS-7. They found no problems in any area. The astronauts were told that they were "go for launch."

Many well-known women had come to watch the STS-7 launch because Sally Ride was on board. Two of them, Margaret Heckler and Elizabeth Dole, were U.S. government officials. Jane Fonda, Gloria Steinem, and other people who were working for women's rights also came to watch the historic flight. For them, Sally showed the progress women were making in performing jobs that had been done before only by men.

For miles around the space center, giant posters and banners said, "Ride, Sally Ride." Dale and Joyce Ride watched from a special visitor's area. Sally's sister, Karen "Bear" Scott, and her husband were with them.

At 31 seconds before lift-off, the computers on board the shuttle took charge of the final countdown. Six seconds before lift-off, the orbiter's three main engines began to burn fuel from the giant orange tank.

A rumbling sound filled the air as white smoke began to curl around the base of the launch platform. Suddenly the solid rocket boosters fired. Large white clouds of smoke swept over the launch platform, and a thunderous roar echoed across the cape.

The spacecraft shook. It seemed to pause for a moment a few feet above the launch pad. Then the white and orange giant zoomed into the blue morning sky.

In less than 30 seconds, the spacecraft was a mile away from the launch site. After two minutes, when the fuel in the twin boosters had burned, the slim tanks broke away and began a parachute glide to earth. Six minutes later,

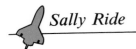

the one and a half million pounds of fuel in the giant orange tank had also been used. The empty tank unhooked from the orbiter and tumbled back to earth. As it entered the atmosphere, it broke up into tiny pieces.

After the launch, ground control of the spacecraft was turned over to the Mission Control Center in Houston. As soon as the astronauts were safely in orbit, the capcom asked the STS-7 crew how it felt to go into space.

"If you've ever been to Disneyland, that was definitely an E ticket!" Sally exclaimed. She was comparing the spaceflight to the park's best rides.

With the excitement of launch behind them, the STS-7 crew settled down to a busy day. Every 90 minutes, *Challenger* completed an orbit of the earth. On the seventh orbit, the crew planned to launch the Anik-C satellite.

Anik-C was a Canadian communications satellite. It would relay voice, pictures, and information services throughout Canada. In the Inuit Indian language, *Anik* means *brother*.

As the seventh orbit drew near, the astronauts prepared to launch the satellite. Bob Crippen and Rick

Hauck opened the orbiter's payload bay doors and slowly turned the shuttle to the correct position. Sally Ride and John Fabian could see into the 60-foot-long cargo bay through the two small windows in the back of the flight deck. Three satellites and two satellite boosters were stored there.

The boosters were needed to push Anik-C and the other communications satellite, Palapa-B, into a higher orbit. *Challenger's* orbit was 160 miles above the earth. Both satellites had to fly at an altitude of 22,300 miles to stay above the same position on the earth.

Sally and John, floating weightless in the flight deck, started the booster rocket spinning. The commander and pilot checked *Challenger's* movement with scientists and computers in Houston. When the shuttle was in position, Sally and John launched the satellite out of the shuttle's payload bay. Rick Hauck moved the orbiter safely away from the spinning satellite. Later, the booster fired, pushing Anik-C into an orbit thousands of miles above the earth.

The five astronauts cheered when mission control told them that the satellite launch was a success. Anik-C

With a thunderous roar, the STS-7 spacecraft lifts off the launch pad at the Kennedy Space Center at Cape Canaveral, Florida.

Like a silent airplane, Challenger *touches down on a runway at Edwards Air Force Base in California.*

An artist's view of the remote manipulator arm lifting the reusable SPAS satellite out of the shuttle's cargo bay.

A happy STS-7 crew aboard Challenger *in space:* (from the left) *Norman Thagard, Commander Robert Crippen, Rick Hauck, Sally Ride, and John Fabian.*

Attached to the remote manipulator arm, the SPAS satellite flies high above the white clouds and blue ocean of the earth far below.

A view of Challenger's *cargo bay in space: the SPAS satellite is nearest the front of the bay, and the remote manipulator arm is at the right.*

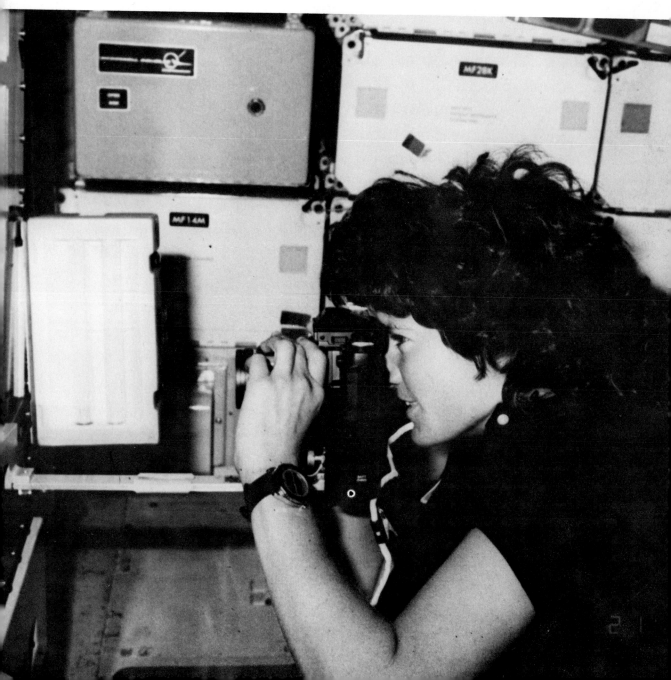

Dr. Sally Ride photographs an experiment in progress aboard Challenger *during the STS-7 mission.*

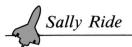

was on the way to its final position. One of the main goals of STS-7 had been met.

Sally and the other crew members could now relax and get ready to sleep. The astronauts didn't need pillows or beds to be comfortable. Weightless in space, they just strapped themselves to places on the walls so they wouldn't bump into anything.

When Sally woke up the next day, sunshine surrounded the spacecraft. She pulled up a window shade and looked out at the earth far below. Just 45 minutes later, *Challenger* passed into darkness as it moved to the night side of the globe. From space, the nations of the world all blended into one another across the oceans and continents of the planet. Looking down, Sally could see the countries she had enjoyed so much as a child.

By the time everyone was awake, the noisy teleprinter was clacking loudly. Every day the five astronauts read the messages that were sent up by mission control and typed on the teleprinter. This morning's message told the space travelers to follow the planned timeline.

Soon it was time for breakfast. Throughout the flight, each of the five crew members took turns preparing their precooked and dried meals. The "chef" for each meal squirted water into sealed plastic pouches to moisten the food. Without gravity, all drinks had to be sipped through a straw from the pouches. Sally thought the many kinds of food and snacks were "pretty good." Between meals, she liked to snack on peanuts.

Early that day Sally Ride and John Fabian prepared to launch a second satellite. Palapa-B was a communications satellite from the Republic of Indonesia. After they had started the booster spinning, the STS-7 mission specialists launched Palapa-B. Meanwhile, Dr. Thagard measured everyone's heart rates and breathing patterns. Once again, mission control told the astronauts that the launch was a success.

The third day in space was the easiest for the five astronauts. If either of the two satellites had not launched on time, NASA had planned to use this day to try again. Since both launches had been a success, the five astronauts had some free time to enjoy.

Sally and the men relaxed and did some exercises. Every day, the crew of the *Challenger* exercised to prepare for returning to the earth's gravity.

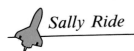

On the next day of the mission, Sally had a lot of experiments to run. For one of them, she checked to see how radish and sunflower seeds would grow without gravity. In the future, the results of this experiment may be used to design large, solar powered space farms.

Another experiment Sally checked on was sent into space by high school students from Camden, New Jersey. This "getaway special" featured an unusual group of space travelers—a colony of carpenter ants. The students wanted to see how weightlessness would change the way the ants behaved.

That evening the STS-7 crew checked the German satellite that would be launched the next day. One part of it, they found, was overheating. Mission control asked the astronauts to go to sleep an hour earlier so that they would have extra time in the morning to check the satellite.

For Sally Ride the fifth day in space was one of the busiest. The timeline called for her and John Fabian to launch and return a satellite using the remote manipulator arm. This challenging job was the most difficult test for the STS-7 crew.

The West German satellite that Sally would move with the arm was called the Shuttle Pallet Satellite, or SPAS. The SPAS was a large, self-contained, space laboratory that could be sent into and returned from space many times. It could be changed to hold a space telescope, instruments to map the earth, or many other things. On this mission, it held eleven experiments.

Mission specialist John Fabian was the first to use the remote manipulator arm. He raised the two-ton SPAS out of the payload bay and released it. Commander Bob Crippen moved the orbiter 1,000 feet away from the German satellite. Two hours later, Bob moved the orbiter closer to the SPAS, and John caught it again with the robot arm.

Now it was Sally's turn to operate the shuttle's strong arm. Carefully, she guided the satellite out of the payload bay and released it. Sally watched the SPAS move in front of the bright, blue-green earth. It looked like a white box kite floating in the black void of space.

The satellite sent live pictures of *Challenger* to NASA tracking stations on earth. It was the first time that the entire orbiter had been photographed flying in space. At one time the crew bent the robot arm into the shape of a giant seven as a sign for the seventh shuttle mission.

Nine hours after the test began, Rick Hauck brought the shuttle back alongside the SPAS. Sally guided the robot arm to the satellite and caught it. She moved it into the payload bay and carefully stored it in its proper place. The SPAS would be the first satellite returned to earth from space.

Sally and her crewmates were thrilled. The three major goals of the flight had been completed.

Commander Crippen claimed proudly, "Some crews in the past have announced that 'We deliver.' Well, from Flight 7, 'We pick up and deliver.' "

NASA scientists were proud of STS-7's success. Learning how the robot arm moved objects in space was an important step toward future missions to repair satellites.

Thursday morning on board *Challenger*, there was much laughter and friendly chatter. The five space travelers ate a hearty breakfast from their plastic pouches.

Bob Crippen radioed to mission control, "We've got five very happy people. This is very exciting up here."

But problems were developing down on earth. NASA had planned for STS-7 to be the first mission to land in Florida, at a site only five miles from the launch pad. Then *Challenger* would not have to make the long trip on top of a 747 jet back to the launch site.

Bad weather was threatening to ruin this plan. Before the astronauts went to sleep, they looked down from space to see clouds swirling over most of Florida. If the weather didn't improve soon, they couldn't land there.

On the morning of their seventh day in space, the STS-7 crew learned that the Kennedy Space Center in Florida was still covered by clouds. Mission control told the astronauts to land at Edwards Air Force Base in California.

Sally, John, Bob, Rick, and Norman strapped themselves into their seats to prepare for their return to earth. The shuttle turned around so that it was flying backwards in space. In this position, firing *Challenger's* engines would slow its speed and cause it to head downward. Computer information from mission control signaled to Bob Crippen and Rick Hauck the exact time to fire the engines. After the firing, the shuttle turned around to fly

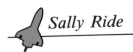

forward again as it plunged through the atmosphere.

For more than 30 minutes, air rushed by *Challenger* so quickly that there could be no radio communication between the orbiter and the ground. Friction caused the spacecraft's protective heat shield to glow red hot. At mission control, NASA officials waited anxiously for the astronauts to radio that they were safely through this "blackout zone."

At last the STS-7 crew broke through on the radio to mission control. By then only 30 minutes remained until landing in California. The capcom gave the astronauts the latest wind speed and direction.

Soon people on the ground at Edwards Air Force Base could see the orbiter as a white dot growing larger and larger in the sky. There weren't many people at the landing site in California's Mojave Desert. Most of those who had wanted to watch the landing, including Sally's parents, were still in Florida.

Like a silent plane, *Challenger* glided through the shimmering desert air. One minute before touchdown, the landing gear unfolded from the underside of the orbiter and locked into place. *Challenger* landed gently on its rear wheels, moving down the runway at 220 miles per hour. As the spacecraft slowed, its nose came down, and the front wheels touched the runway.

People cheered as *Challenger* came to a stop. The flight had lasted 6 days, 2 hours, and 24 minutes and had made 98 orbits around the earth. Everything except the attempt to land in Florida had worked perfectly. The mission was a smashing success!

6/"Now It's Possible"

Dr. Sally Ride, America's first woman in space, was showered with praise from people all over the world. Sally wanted the other members of the STS-7 crew to get their share of praise, too. When she received invitations that did not include the other crew members, she turned them down.

At a postflight news conference, Sally told reporters, "The thing that I'll remember most about the flight is that it was fun. I'm sure that it was the most fun that I'll ever have in my life."

After her flight, Sally spoke to many groups about her experiences as an astronaut. She spoke to young people in schools and colleges and to state governors and state legislatures. Most of all, she enjoyed talking to girls and boys who wanted to know what it was like to fly in space.

"That's one of the things that's most gratifying about

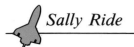

the public part of this job," Sally said. "When I go out and give talks at schools and an eight-year-old girl in the audience raises her hand to ask me what she needs to do to become an astronaut, I like that. It's neat!

"Because now there really is a way. Now it's possible."

Sally toured Europe and spoke to many groups there. She also addressed a session of the United Nations in New York City. Everywhere Sally went, she described what her flight was like and encouraged young girls and women to become scientists or astronauts.

In November 1983, NASA announced that Sally Ride was scheduled for a second spaceflight in early 1985. Sally is looking forward to soaring skyward again. "I came into this because I wanted to fly in space," she said before the STS-7 mission. "My intention after the flight is to come back to the astronaut office and get back in line and try to fly again. I'd like to do it as many times as NASA will let me."

Before Sally's second spaceflight, her husband, Steven Hawley, flew on his first in August 1984. On the first flight of the shuttle orbiter *Discovery*, Steven was a mission specialist. When asked before the flight what she had said to her husband, Sally replied, "Steven doesn't need any advice from me."

Sally and Steve live in a comfortable three bedroom home not far from Johnson Space Center. The two astronauts plan to continue their spacebound work as long as NASA needs them. Usually Sally has refused to answer questions about her married life. She has said, though, that she and Steven do not plan to have children.

Perhaps Sally remembers the one and only time she baby-sat. When she made peanut butter and jelly sandwiches for the children, they refused to eat them. The peanut butter and jelly, said the kids, were in the wrong order. Angered, Sally threw out the sandwiches and made new ones for the children. After that she never baby-sat again.

Since Sally Ride first flew in space, she has received many awards and honors. One of them was a 1984 Jefferson Award for public service, which she accepted in a Washington, D.C., ceremony. Whatever Sally decides to do in the future, she has already done much to be proud of aboard the *Challenger*. In space and on earth, Sally Ride has been a challenger of life.

Glossary

astronaut—a person trained to work in space

astronomy—the study of space and the objects in space

atmosphere—the layer of gases above the surface of a planet or star

Cape Canaveral—the main site for America's space launches; it is located in the Kennedy Space Center

Challenger—the name of the second space shuttle orbiter

Columbia—the name of the first space shuttle orbiter

engineer—a person trained to apply scientific discoveries to solve practical problems

gravity—the force by which all objects pull on all other objects. Gravity is what makes the planets go around the sun

Johnson Space Center—the Houston space center in charge of astronaut crew training and mission control

Kennedy Space Center—the Florida space center in charge of U.S. spacecraft launches

meteorology—the study of weather and climate

Mission Control Center—the part of Johnson Space Center responsible for managing spacecraft during missions

mission specialist—a space shuttle astronaut trained to work with payloads

NASA—the National Aeronautics and Space Administration, a U.S. government agency in charge of space programs

orbit—the path that an object, such as a satellite, follows as it moves around another object, such as the earth

payload—cargo, including satellites and experiments, carried into space by the shuttle and other spacecraft

physics—the study of the physical laws of nature

Project Apollo—the U.S. space program that sent astronauts to the moon

Project Gemini—the U.S. space program that sent astronauts into space to gather information needed for Project Apollo

Project Mercury—the first U.S. program to send astronauts into space; Project Mercury missions gathered information needed for Project Gemini

remote manipulator system—a 50-foot robot arm and its controls located in the shuttle orbiter's payload bay. The arm can be used to launch satellites in space and return them to the orbiter's payload bay

satellites—used here to describe human-made objects that orbit the earth and relay information to the ground

shuttle simulator—equipment designed to look and act like a space shuttle orbiter and used for practice sessions

solid rocket boosters—on the space shuttle, two slim rockets filled with powerful propellants which provide extra power during launch

space—officially defined as the area more than fifty miles above the earth's surface where there is no atmosphere

Space Transportation System (STS)—the parts of the space shuttle—an orbiter, a 154-foot fuel tank, and two solid rocket boosters

T-38—a jet holding a pilot and one passenger which is used in flight training

timeline—a planned schedule of activities

X rays—powerful, invisible waves of energy given off by some materials in special places, such as the atmospheres of stars

 *Index*

The Author

Carolyn Blacknall is an Operations Integration Officer at Mission Control in NASA's Johnson Space Center in Houston, Texas. Her job involves the coordination of mission operations during space shuttle flights and simulations. The author served for two years as editor-in-chief of *NASA Network,* a publication of the space center. Her education includes a B.A. in astronomy and an M.S. in aerospace engineering from the University of Texas, where she studied the orbit of the LAGEOS satellite.

   Ms. Blacknall is a member of the American Institute of Aeronautics and Astronautics, the Texas Society of Professional Engineers, and the Federal Women's Program Committee. She lives in Houston with her husband and two children.